To: Callen

You're a
Great Friend
and Walking/Soul
Companion!

Jack

# JACK ULDRICH

A FUTURIST'S **UN**ORTHODOX, **UN**CONVENTIONAL,
AND **UN**COMFORTABLE GUIDE TO DOING BUSINESS

# BUSINESS AS UNUSUAL

RIVER GROVE
BOOKS

Published by River Grove Books
Austin, TX
www.rivergrovebooks.com

Distributed by River Grove Books

Design and composition by Greenleaf Book Group
Cover design by Greenleaf Book Group
Cover Images: ©iStockphoto/fizkes, ©iStockphoto/Adene Sanchez, ©iStockphoto/eternalcreative, and ©iStockphoto/Rawpixel

Publisher's Cataloging-in-Publication data is available.

Print ISBN: 978-1-63299-309-0

eBook ISBN: 978-1-63299-310-6

First Edition

# PREFACE

A book titled *Business as Unusual* can't be written as a typical business book. Most books in this genre are between fifty thousand and sixty-five thousand words, and are designed to be read in five hours—about the length of a cross-country flight. This is nonsense.

The world of business is changing fast, and business books must adapt as well.

Therefore, I have written this book to be succinct. If a quote, picture, chart, or story sufficed to make my point, I left it at that. My goal is for you to be able to digest the contents of this book in less than an hour.

Enjoy!

# AUTHOR'S NOTE

This book was originally scheduled for publication in April of 2020. The global pandemic struck in force in March of 2020. All of the lessons contained in this book are still relevant—perhaps even more so now—but, in some cases, for different reasons.

In order to get this book into publication as quickly as possible for the purpose of helping individuals, businesses, and corporations navigate these "unusual" times, I have made only minor changes to the text but, where appropriate, I have acknowledged the pandemic.

As a leader, however, it is also important to understand that while COVID-19 will change many things, it will also accelerate many of the trends outlined and described in this book.

# I LOVE THIS CARTOON FROM THE CREATOR OF *F MINUS*, TONY CARRILLO.

First, I'm not a business "guru" and don't claim to be. I'm more about delivering those "AHA moments." And here is my big "AHA":

AHA is an acronym. It stands for awareness, humility, and action.

To navigate the future, today's business leaders must

- be **AWARE** of how technological , economic, social, cultural, and political trends are accelerating, burgeoning, and converging

- have **HUMILITY** to the idea that what worked yesterday might not be sufficient tomorrow

- take **ACTION** to create a new and better future

# AHA #1:
## WHY BUSINESS AS *UN*USUAL IS NOW USUAL

un usual

PAST        FUTURE

# IN THE WORLD OF BUSINESS, *UN*USUAL WILL BE THE NEW USUAL.

Don't believe me?

Consider the following:

- Within a month of COVID-19 being declared a national emergency, 51 percent of the workforce began working remotely—demonstrating business can change quickly when needed.

- Twitter told its employees that they could work from home—forever!

- In the first two months of the pandemic, e-commerce sales doubled. Stated another way, in eight weeks, internet sales increased as much as in the past ten years combined.

- Airline traffic had declined to levels not seen since the 1950s and hotel vacancy rates were at historic lows, but jigsaw puzzle sales went through the roof.

- But even prior to COVID-19, the world was changing rapidly.

- In early 2020, more consumers were already having more meals delivered to them than were dining out.

- Growing up, many of us were told by our mothers, "Never get into a car with a stranger." Today, the advice is routinely ignored billions of times a year thanks to Uber and Lyft.

- Millions of people were swapping hotels for the beds of strangers because of Airbnb.

- A private citizen has launched a rocket into outer space—and returned it safely back to earth. Two other billionaires are pursuing similar plans, and one plans to launch tourists into space by 2021.

- Waymo's autonomous vehicles have logged over fifteen million miles of road experience, making the company's software and artificial intelligence "the most experienced driver in the world." Within the past two years, tens of millions of consumers have put AI—in the form of the Amazon Echo and Google Home—into their homes. Concerned that their children are learning poor social skills because of how they interact with the smart speakers, some parents have programmed their devices to respond only when their kids have prefaced their requests with the word "please."

- Some chatbots are now so good that many humans can't tell when they are speaking to a computer. In other words, people are now having *natural* conversations with *artificial* intelligence.

- One of the people on *Time* magazine's list of the "25 Most Influential People on the Internet," Lil Miquela, isn't a person. It's an avatar with over 1.5 million human followers.

- A Jimmy Buffett–themed "Margaritaville" senior housing complex has opened in Florida. With continued advances in biotechnology, regenerative medicine, and stem cell research, people claim that fifty is the new thirty, seventy is the new fifty, and soon one hundred may be the new seventy. If true, today's seniors might be "wasting away in Margaritaville" for decades more to come.

- Robots are doing backflips, drones are delivering medical supplies, and hundreds of workers are donning soft robotic exoskeletons to enhance their strength and avoid injuries. Some exoskeletons can even shape-shift into "chairless chairs."

- Google has developed an affordable voice translation device and is deploying high-altitude balloons in the hopes of delivering high-speed internet access everywhere on the planet by 2024. The combination suggests that people may soon be able to communicate with all eight billion of the world's inhabitants in their native tongue.

- A student at MIT has created a brain-computer interface device that allows him to access the internet by thought alone, and the Pentagon has figured out how to allow soldiers to control a swarm of drones by employing related technologies.

- Walmart has filed a patent for a virtual shopping experience, while Amazon has filed one for an airborne fulfillment center. If the former works, a person will be able to virtually stroll down a store aisle and select whatever goods they want. If the latter works, those goods could be dropped from a giant blimp and delivered via a drone directly to your doorstep.

- According to the World Economic Forum, 65 percent of kindergartners beginning school today will work in jobs that don't yet exist.

- A venture capital firm has appointed an algorithm to its board of directors.

- Tesla, which didn't even exist fifteen years ago, is now twice as valuable as General Motors; and Ford says it is no longer an automobile company but rather "a mobility provider."

- Major colleges and universities are offering scholarships for "eSports"—electronic sports. The National Basketball Association has started an eSport league, and the Olympic Committee has indicated it expects eSports to be sanctioned as Olympic sports as early as 2024. (If COVID-19 keeps people from physical events, this trend could accelerate even faster.)

- In South Korea, there are more virtual golfers than there are golfers.

- The former president of Yale University is now the president of Coursera, which offers MOOCs—massive open online courses.

- Amazon, which was once putting bookstores out of business, has opened its own physical bookstores. It has also created its first cashierless store and plans to open three thousand more by 2021—yet another trend that could accelerate as a result of the world moving to "contactless commerce" in the wake of the global pandemic.

- Some companies are embedding microchips in their employees ("voluntarily"), others are working on bloodless blood tests and anti-aging pills, and still others have produced prototypes of flying cars and have plans to deploy them as early as 2022.

- Self-healing concrete, man-made diamonds, gluten-free wheat, animal-free milk, and "real" vegan cheese are now all actual products.

- Things are getting so *un*usual that the world's largest meat companies are now investing in artificial meat, and McDonald's and Burger King are serving "plant-based protein."

Such *un*usual moments will only become more usual in the future for one simple reason:

If there is one thing you must understand about the future, it is that not only is the world changing; the rate of change is increasing at an exponential pace.

If you don't grasp this basic concept, you will be out of business sooner than you think.

Most people claim to understand exponential growth, but they don't. If you take only one thing away from this book, let it be this: Study exponential growth, understand exponential growth, and internalize exponential growth.

The following chart is your new reality, and various versions of it will be repeated throughout this book because the concept is of the utmost importance and provides the foundation for much of the book's *un*usual advice.

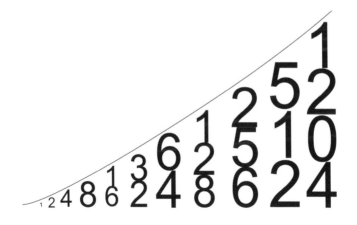

Here's why: Due to the power of exponential growth, if a technology's capabilities double ten times, it will be a thousand times larger than when it started.

Here are some real-world examples:

The most appropriate, relevant, and top-of-mind example of exponential growth is, of course, a viral pandemic. Early on, a doubling might not look significant as it moves from two to four to eight. But as the doubling continues and more people become sick, with the numbers moving into the thousands and then the millions, it becomes almost like a freight train force incapable of being easily controlled.

Adidas 3D-printed five thousand shoes in 2018. If that number doubles every year, the company will be printing ten million shoes in a decade's time and the global supply chain will never be the same.

**2020:** 20,000          **2025:** 640,000

**2021:** 40,000          **2026:** 1,280,000

**2022:** 80,000          **2027:** 2,560,000

**2023:** 160,000         **2028:** 5,120,000

**2024:** 320,000         **2029:** 10,240,000

Solar power currently produces approximately 2 percent of the world's electricity needs. But if that number doubles every two years (which is possible), it would grow to more than 100 percent by 2032. If this happens, the world of energy and geopolitics will never be the same. Don't believe me? Here's the math:

**2022:** 4%
**2024:** 8%
**2026:** 16%
**2028:** 32%
**2030:** 64%
**2032:** 128%

If genomic sequencing technology continues to double in capacity for the foreseeable future—as is expected— gene sequencing might not only get one thousand times faster, but it could also fall to a thousandth of the cost. If this occurs, the agriculture, health-care, and pharmaceutical industries will never be the same. Here's what happens if you cut a thousand dollars in half every year:

| | |
|---|---|
| **2020:** $1,000 | **2025:** $31.25 |
| **2021:** $500 | **2026:** $15.63 |
| **2022:** $250 | **2027:** $7.81 |
| **2023:** $125 | **2028:** $3.90 |
| **2024:** $62.50 | **2029:** $1.95 |

In the coming decade, the amount of data collected (from everything from our DNA to information from trillions of sensors) is expected to increase from

WE AREN'T JUST
LIVING IN AN
**ERA OF CHANGE.**
WE ARE IN A
**CHANGE OF ERA.**

exabytes—one quintillion, or 1,000,000,000,000,000,000 bytes—to zettabytes and then to yottabytes. A zettabyte is a thousand times larger than an exabyte, and a yottabyte is a thousand times larger than a zettabyte. This means the amount of collected data will increase a millionfold.

Cloud computing was facilitated by yesteryear's increases in data storage from terabytes to exabytes and was harnessed by innovative entrepreneurs and business professionals to reinvent the retail, supply chain, health-care, and energy industries. Is it not possible that next-generation entrepreneurs and business people will also figure out how to exploit the coming exponential increase in data to transform banking, energy, farming, health care, retail, and manufacturing?

If you can't contemplate this reality, you need to wake up!

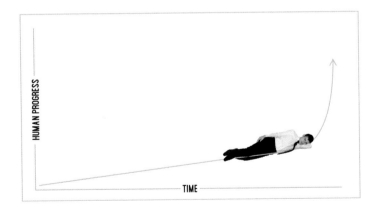

ONE REASON EVEN **SMART PEOPLE MISS THE FUTURE** IS BECAUSE THEY FAIL TO APPRECIATE THAT OUR TOOLS ARE BECOMING EXPONENTIALLY MORE POWERFUL.

# HUMILITY
## BEWARE OF THE DAY AFTER TOMORROW

The proper way to understand exponential growth is to grasp this idea: The next doubling—say the eleventh doubling of any trend—is equal to every previous step combined plus one.

For example, today's most powerful supercomputer is capable of a mind-boggling 200 quintillion calculations per second. It is being used to solve some of the world's most complex problems in material science, weather forecasting, and drug discovery.

And yet the next supercomputer will soon be capable of 400 quintillion calculations per second, which is equal to today's most powerful supercomputer and all the supercomputers created since 1948—combined!

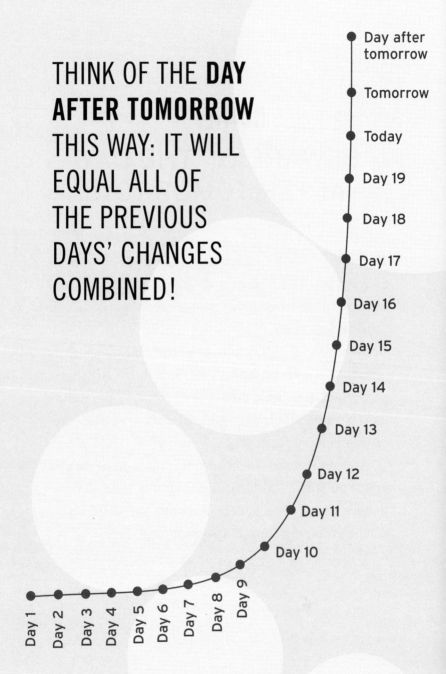

THINK OF THE **DAY AFTER TOMORROW** THIS WAY: IT WILL EQUAL ALL OF THE PREVIOUS DAYS' CHANGES COMBINED!

Day after tomorrow

Tomorrow

Today

Day 19

Day 18

Day 17

Day 16

Day 15

Day 14

Day 13

Day 12

Day 11

Day 10

Day 9

Day 8

Day 7

Day 6

Day 5

Day 4

Day 3

Day 2

Day 1

Trends do not continue to double forever. Every trend ultimately reaches some limit. Consider, for example, Moore's Law—an observation made in 1965 by Intel cofounder Gordon Moore that the number of transistors that could fit on a chip was doubling every year or two. This pattern fueled the exponential growth of computing power over the past half century and was instrumental in the creation of both the personal computer and internet revolutions. But sometime within the next ten years, it will reach its limit.

Quantum computing may pick up the baton, and it is likely that society will see existing 32-qubit quantum computers grow exponentially. And these radical advances will make today's supercomputers seem as quaint as a dial-up modem or rotary phone.

More importantly, quantum computers may help solve some of today's most vexing scientific problems and could lead to *un*precedented developments in everything from better batteries and next-generation super materials to innovative new drugs, including drugs and vaccines for the next pandemic.

YOU CAN'T
INCREMENTALIZE
YOURSELF OR YOUR
COMPANY INTO
THE FUTURE.

# ACTION
## THINK 10X, NOT 10%

Katerra, a new start-up in the construction industry, is striving to build buildings in two weeks instead of twenty—a tenfold improvement. Elon Musk, the CEO of SpaceX, is seeking to lower the cost of launching a satellite into space by 90 percent. And Minerva, an innovative university, is seeking to provide an Ivy League education for one-tenth the cost of a real Ivy League education.

As a leader, it's time to *un*constrain your thoughts and set *un*reasonable goals. Ask yourself the following questions:

How would your business change if you had ten times as many customers?

What if you could build your products for a tenth of the price?

What if you could offer your customers a tenfold improvement in convenience, efficiency, or cost?

These seem like impossible tasks, but they're not.

Think harder about the trends transforming your business today and tomorrow. Your competitors are! And if they aren't, some entrepreneur in some distant corner of the world is—guaranteed.

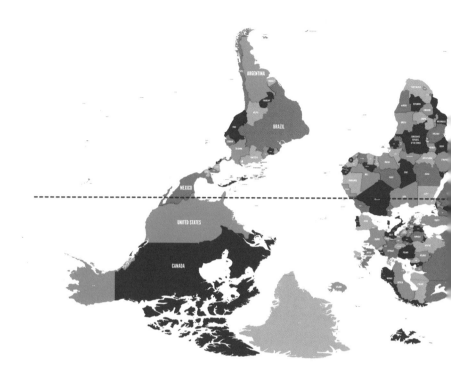

# *UN*USUAL TIP 1
# DOWN IS THE NEW UP

Fifty percent of the world's population is under the age of thirty—and most of them live on the top portion of this *un*usual map.

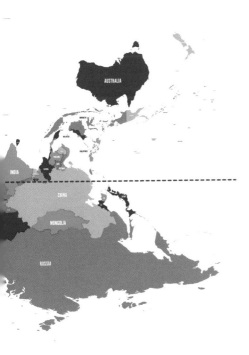

Moreover, in the next few years, three billion additional people will get access to high-speed internet connections, smartphones, mobile banking apps, affordable capital, high-quality online education, clean water, renewable energy, healthier food, and better preventative health-care services. The opportunity for global growth will be extraordinary.

Keep the map above in mind when you need to be reminded that the *un*usual will only become more usual—because 90 percent of the world's next entrepreneurs, start-ups, and small businesses are going to come from the top half of this upside-down map.

# AHA #2:
## EXPLORE THE
## *UN*KNOWN

PAST    FUTURE

## NO ONE WOULD DISPUTE THAT JOHANNES GUTENBERG'S PRINTING PRESS WAS A REVOLUTIONARY DEVELOPMENT.

Gutenberg's genius was not that he created the device out of thin air. Rather, he combined four existing technologies—a wine press, moveable type, ink, and paper—into a device that changed the world.

The world of tomorrow will not be created out of thin air either. It will come from the convergence of a wide variety of accelerating technologies.

A contemporary example of convergence can be found in ride-sharing apps. Ten years ago, smartphones, GPS technology, and cloud computing all existed. As of 2010, no one had yet converged the three technologies into a platform that allowed people to safely, affordably, and conveniently catch rides with strangers.

In this same vein, tomorrow's *un*usual, *un*conventional, and *un*thinkable companies will be created from sensor technology, big data, cloud computing, artificial intelligence, 5G networks, synthetic biology, genomics, 3D printing, and robotics.

These technologies will converge to make the physical world around us "smart." Billions and then trillions of sensors will collect zettabytes and then yottabytes of data. This data will then be uploaded to the cloud (and edge computing platforms), where sophisticated algorithms will cull out valuable and actionable insights.

Artificial intelligence will be everywhere. It will be the new electricity, and consumers and citizens will simply expect their devices, homes, roads, buildings, and cities to be intelligent and interact with them in new, faster, and more meaningful ways. Many problems will be prevented before they even occur.

Other companies will converge robotics, 3D printers, and new advances in material science to transform the manufacturing world.

Still others will leverage genomics, synthetic biology, and blockchain technology to transform the agriculture, healthcare, and pharmaceutical industries by further merging the physical and digital worlds.

Things will then get really *un*usual because existing technologies will converge with emerging technologies—including quantum computing, satellite technology, renewable energy, massive open online courses, gene editing, and augmented and virtual reality—to further revolutionize the world.

One way to think of the vast world of opportunity that awaits is to think in terms of combinations. If fourteen technological platforms exist, that doesn't mean there are fourteen new ways of doing business; instead it means a mind-boggling eighty-seven billion possible combinations exist (1 x 2 x 3 x 4 x 5 x 6 x 7 x 8 x 9 x 10 x 11 x 12 x 13 x 14 = 87,178,291,200).

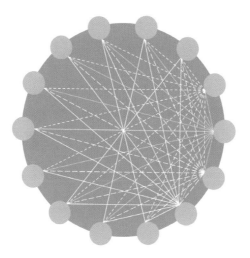

Now, many of these possibilities will be repetitive, ridiculous, ineffective, *un*helpful, or *un*usable. By the same token, it would be foolish to think that someone, somewhere on this vast planet won't think of a better way to design, build, deliver, or produce whatever product or service from which you currently derive your livelihood.

# AWARENESS
## THE *UN*KNOWN IS MORE IMPORTANT THAN THE KNOWN

Before the entire globe was mapped, cartographers placed dragons on *un*mapped portions of the world. The dragons denoted "known *un*knowns." In this same spirit, business leaders must also beware of dragons. These "dragons" could be emerging technologies, shifting customer preferences and tastes, or *un*expected game-changing world events, such as wars, terrorist attacks, pandemics, or natural disasters.

## HC SVNT DRACONES

**HUMILITY**
YOUR IGNORANCE IS
GROWING FASTER
THAN YOUR KNOWLEDGE

● Known
*un*Known

# ACTION
## RESEARCH AND REFLECT

Pick just one trend that you consider *un*stoppable—5G, sensor technology, big data, AI, blockchain, quantum computing, nanotechnology, robotics, 3D printing, biotechnology, synthetic biology, renewable energy, augmented reality, virtual reality, satellite technology, genomics, gene editing, online education, etc.—and research how it is already impacting your industry. Then reflect on how your business could change even more in the near future.

# UNUSUAL TIP 2
# START AN ANTI-LIBRARY

An anti-library is a shelf of books that the owner has not yet read. It is designed to grow ever larger, and its purpose is to serve as a constant reminder of one's ignorance.

Also, always remember this: "The absence of evidence is not evidence of absence." (If this quote doesn't make sense, re-read it until it does. The failure to grasp its wisdom is one of the primary reasons individuals and businesses are so often caught unprepared; they think that just because something *has* not happened that it *can't* happen.)

# AHA #3:
## *UN*LOCK FAILURE

PAST    FUTURE

## TO GET OVER A FEAR OF MISTAKES,

a number of rug weavers purposely place an error in their rugs at the beginning of the weaving process.

This *un*orthodox action has the benefit of enhancing their skills. Because they are no longer obsessively focused on perfection, they produce more rugs and, as a result, each successive rug tends to improve in quality.

# AWARENESS
## FAILURE IS THE KEY TO *UN*LOCKING SUCCESS

In today's accelerating world, strategic planning is becoming less helpful. This is because it can lull business leaders into a false sense of security by causing them to believe the future is more plannable than it really is—a fact that the 2020 global pandemic made abundantly clear to most businesses.

If strategic planning is less useful, what replaces it? Strategic experimentation.

Since no one knows for certain what will work in the future, business leaders must get more comfortable with the idea of strategic experimentation.

Consider this example: Before the US put a man into space, NASA launched twelve monkeys. Many of those monkeys didn't return safely. But the lessons we learned from those failures ultimately made it safer to launch astronauts into space.

Businesses can—and must—do the same. Consider, for example, WD-40. It only became a success after the first thirty-nine attempts at creating a water-displacement formula failed.

What experiments might you undertake today to better position your business for tomorrow's rapidly changing world?

"Only the hand that can erase, can unlock failure.

THE **RISKIEST**
**THING** TO DO
IS PLAY IT SAFE.

# HUMILITY
## *UN*BREAKABLE RULES ARE MEANT TO BE BROKEN

Ernst & Young now hires professional employees with no university degrees.

Airbnb ignores the rules that apply to hotels.

Uber and Lyft do the same with taxi regulations.

Amazon "fires" some of its customers.

Zappos pays employees $2,000 to leave after only two weeks of training if they are not a good cultural fit for the company.

Intel has a "no email" policy on Fridays.

Tyson Foods, North America's largest meat producer, is investing in artificial meat.

> " Hell, there are no rules here. We're trying to accomplish something. "
>
> —Thomas Edison

# ACTION
## PLAY IT *UN*SAFE

One CEO has an annual "Heroic Failure" award. It is awarded to a person, team, idea, product, or service that was well conceived but didn't work. Similarly, another CEO who knows his own penchant for "punishing" failure provides every employee two Get Out of Jail Free cards; if an employee's idea doesn't work and the CEO seeks to mete out punishment to him or her, all the employee needs to do is present the card to the CEO.

Both actions send powerful messages that the leaders are serious about innovating, experimenting, and taking risks. They accept that failure is an integral component of moving forward and, instead, create an environment where "*un*safe" thinking and failure are encouraged, recognized, and rewarded.

At your workplace, experiment with ways to reward failure and encourage employees to play it "unsafe."

THE RULES ARE **CHANGING.**

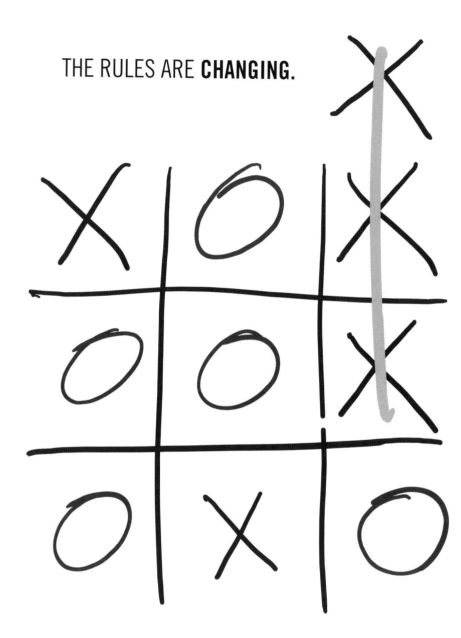

WHO SAYS SOMEONE
CAN'T—AND WON'T—DO
IT ANOTHER WAY?

# UNUSUAL TIP 3
## STANDING IS THE
## NEW SITTING

Hold your next meeting standing up. Not only is standing healthier than sitting, but people are also less willing to pontificate when everyone is standing.

Standing has the added benefit of making people *un*comfortable. As a result, it tends to focus people's minds and move them to action that much faster.

# AHA #4:
## EXPECT THE *UN*EXPECTED

un

expected

un

PAST    FUTURE

# IN A NOW INFAMOUS 2009 VIDEO,

Steve Ballmer, then CEO of Microsoft, arrogantly dismisses Apple's new iPhone because it "costs five hundred dollars and doesn't have a keyboard."

It is easy to laugh at Ballmer, but the clip should instead serve as a warning to every business leader: Don't *un*derestimate technology.

One hundred years ago, a majority of Americans derived their livelihood from farming.

Fifty years ago, massive computers were being run on punch cards.

Thirty years ago, cell phones cost $5,000.

Twenty years ago, people connected to the internet via 56k dial-up modems.

Ten years ago, people were still hailing taxis with their arms.

Five years ago, Netflix was just getting into "content production."

And less than a year ago, the possibility of a pandemic throwing the global economy into a tailspin seemed too remote to warrant a thought.

WE TEND TO **OVERESTIMATE**
THE EFFECT OF TECHNOLOGY
IN THE SHORT RUN
AND ***UN*DERESTIMATE** THE EFFECT
IN THE LONG RUN.

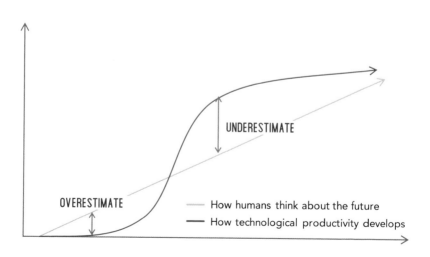

UNDERESTIMATE

OVERESTIMATE

—— How humans think about the future
—— How technological productivity develops

# AWARENESS
## CONTEMPLATE WHAT'S NEXT

As a business leader, you must be aware of what is coming next. Do not get caught *un*aware of accelerating trends in artificial intelligence, battery technology, blockchain technology, fusion power, quantum computing, urban agriculture, voice translation technology, satellites, renewable energy, or autonomous vehicles. Something new is coming. I can't tell you exactly what it is, and that's why you must stay vigilant and aware.

Who thought, for example, that a viral disease could drive every university and college student to online learning in a matter of weeks or that airline traffic could plummet 95 percent in less than a month?

# HUMILITY
## OBJECTS IN THE MIRROR ARE CLOSER THAN *UN*EXPECTED

In the 1980s, AT&T hired consultants to forecast the adoption of mobile phones. Those "experts" predicted there would only be 900,000 cell phones by the year 2000. The number turned out to be 109 million. They were wrong by a factor of 120, and AT&T missed the initial wave of the smartphone revolution.

It might be easy to dismiss the consultants' wildly inaccurate predictions as a one-time affair, but they weren't. For twelve straight years, the International Energy Agency also *un*derestimated the growth of solar power. For twelve straight years, it predicted linear growth. For twelve straight years, it was wrong. If you were wildly wrong for twelve years, wouldn't you revisit your models, your assumptions, and your estimates of a technology? Wouldn't you have humility?

Conservative projections are not always wrong, but when they are they can be very wrong. Do not get lulled by "safe" projections.

(One day a trend, such as a viral disease, can seem under control and a week later it can be out of control.)

# ACTION
## BET ON CHEAP

Emerging technologies may not revolutionize the business world tomorrow, but they will transform it sooner than many people expect. Therefore, anticipate cheapness. One of the corollaries of exponential growth is that some—but not all—things affected by exponential growth get dramatically less expensive.

When data storage got cheap enough, cloud computing became practical and many IT functions were suddenly outsourced.

When bandwidth transitioned from 3G to 4G, new mobile apps suddenly became possible and the price of catching a ride to the airport dropped significantly.

What will happen when 4G transitions to 5G? What might become feasible? How might your business change? How might the expectations of your customers change?

What will happen when 3D printers get so good and affordable that manufacturers can produce most objects in close proximity to the customer?

What will happen when solar becomes cheaper than coal, nuclear, and natural gas?

What will happen when it costs more to flush a toilet than to sequence a human genome?

What will happen when advances in vertical farming become so efficient that growing fresh produce in an urban setting becomes more economic, convenient, and sustainable than on a traditional farm located hundreds or thousands of miles away from the end customer?

# UNUSUAL TIP 4
# BEWARE OF "PHASE CHANGES"

Normally, a drop in the temperature of one degree—say from 80 degrees to 79 degrees—is scarcely noticeable. But when the temperature changes from 33 degrees to 32 degrees, water turns to ice. It experiences a phase change, and it is a material difference.

The same is true in business. Don't believe me?

The most recent example, of course, is COVID-19. When exactly the virus got on an airplane and departed Wuhan isn't exactly known, but the world changed that day. It underwent a "phase change."

Consider the cautionary tale of the price of a New York City taxi medallion—a regulatory device designed to limit the number of taxis that can operate in the city. When, precisely, the convergence of GPS technology, smartphones, and cloud computing got so good that the "conditions" for hailing a ride changed is hard to pinpoint, but almost overnight, ride-sharing services such as Uber and Lyft were able to bypass those regulations, and between 2014 and 2017, the price of a taxi medallion fell from $1,000,000 to less than $200,000.

AVERAGE NYC TAXI MEDALLION PRICES, JAN. 2008 TO JUNE 2017

Or consider this future scenario: Advances in car battery technology improve so much that the number of customers demanding electric vehicles soars. As this happens, the demand for fuel goes down. As the demand for fuel goes down, the demand for ethanol goes down. As the demand for ethanol goes down, the demand for corn goes down. As the demand for corn goes down, the demand for farmland plummets and so do land prices.

Conditions can change fast. Be aware. When—and how—might your business experience a phase change?

# AHA #5:
## *UN*LEARNING IS AS IMPORTANT AS LEARNING

un learn

PAST    FUTURE

**"** The future belongs
to those who can
learn, unlearn,
and relearn. **"**

—Alvin Toffler

# AWARENESS
## BE AWARE OF
## *UN*SEEN KNOWLEDGE

Scientific, medical, and technological knowledge is doubling approximately every five years. This implies that everything we know today—which is a lot—will only represent the tip of the iceberg in the near future. Much of this yet-to-be-created knowledge will require society to *un*learn some of the things it knows today.

BEWARE
OF THE
*UN*KNOWN

"I cannot conceive of any vital disaster happening to this vessel.
—Edward Smith, Captain, *Titanic*

# HUMILITY
## *UN*SEEN THINGS CAN SINK *UN*SINKABLE SHIPS

Knowledge is useless unless you know where it ends.

We don't know what we don't know. This sounds obvious, and it is, but it is a hard idea to grasp.

Captain Smith of the RMS *Titanic* said, "I cannot conceive of any vital disaster happening to this vessel." Smith didn't know what he didn't know. He thought that just because he couldn't conceive of a threat to his ship it was safe.

Have humility. No product, no service, no business, no economy—no matter how big or successful—is "*un*sinkable." Remember Sears? The "everything store" of yesteryear? Now it's bankrupt.

A more contemporary example is COVID-19. It's too soon know the full extent of its impact, but a number of businesses, including retailers, airlines, hotels, universities, and commercial real estate properties, which may have previously considered themselves "unsinkable," will be "sunk" by a tiny virus.

To avoid a similar fate in the future, every business must understand that resilience is often as important as efficiency and profits, and that long-term viability isn't always defined by financial success—sometimes it is defined by the ability to survive.

# ACTION
## STRIVE TO SEE
## THE *UN*SEEN

Take a look at this familiar corporate logo. Do you notice anything *un*usual?

It is difficult to see the *un*seen, but hidden threats and opportunities are staring us in the face every day.

Do you see the arrow between the "E" and the "X"?

Once the arrow is pointed out, it is difficult to *un*see.

But how do you, as a business leader, *un*learn the idea that your vision isn't as good as you think it is? A good place to start is by appointing a chief *un*learning officer. This individual's primary job is to challenge assumptions, question the *un*questionable, think the *un*thinkable, see the *un*seen, and listen to the *un*heard.

Their primary responsibility is to make sure you and your business are not caught *un*aware—by anything.

Can't afford such a position within your company or organization? *Un*learn your current job description and assume the job of CUO yourself.

# **UN**USUAL TIP 5

## CLIMB THE "**UN**LEARNING CURVE" BY ASKING QUESTIONS

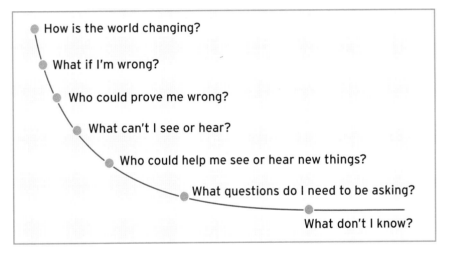

How is the world changing?

What if I'm wrong?

Who could prove me wrong?

What can't I see or hear?

Who could help me see or hear new things?

What questions do I need to be asking?

What don't I know?

# AHA #6:
## YOU NEED TO GET COMFORTABLE BEING *UN*COMFORTABLE

*un*comfortable

PAST    FUTURE

# FOR YEARS, I'VE BEEN A RUNNER.

For years, I've ignored the importance of stretching. Now that I'm older, I've come to appreciate the importance of stretching and cross-training. The reason for my reluctance was simple: I was comfortable running. So why would I change? The strategy of doing what I had always done the day before had worked well my entire life.

Alas, what kept me in shape in my youth no longer suffices. I have recently had to get comfortable being *un*comfortable—doing yoga, using a pilates reformer, swimming, and cross-country skiing.

The same is true in business. You are likely successful because you have perfected a way of doing business. Unfortunately, what worked yesterday won't necessarily work in the future—especially in a world of accelerating change.

Therefore you must begin stretching yourself into new and uncomfortable conditions. After all, a business's "comfort zone" can only expand by moving out into new and uncomfortable spaces, products, services, or territories.

" It all goes back to improv.
You have to get comfortable
being uncomfortable. "

—Amy Poehler

# AWARENESS
## SCARY THINGS ARE WORTHWHILE

Doing something new is often scary but, as my mother said to me years ago, "If something both excites you and scares you, it is probably worth doing."

If you are looking for inspiration, try to recall the feeling you had on the first day of school when you later met one of your best friends, or the feeling in your stomach the first time you mustered up the courage to speak to your future spouse or partner, or even the pain of failing at an activity that later became a favorite hobby. Remember, courage isn't the absence of fear, it is the ability to act in spite of the feeling of fear.

"Feel the fear, but do it anyways!"

—Susan Jeffers

# HUMILITY
## THERE IS AN *I* IN TEAM

We have grown up hearing the cliché that there is no *i* in *team*. Well, that is wrong! (Turn the page!)

If you want to get *un*comfortable, find the "missing i's": Hire innovative, imaginative, independent, iconoclastic, intelligent, and inquisitive individuals who will challenge assumptions, question the status quo, and otherwise bring up *un*usual and *un*comfortable ideas and suggestions. These individuals are also more likely to seek out *un*shared information, find *un*discovered paths, and conjure up *un*imagined alternatives. As a result, these individuals are going to expand your mind, widen your horizons, and push the boundaries of what you may think is prudent, wise, or even possible.

# ACTION
## GET INTO YOUR DISCOMFORT ZONE

Specifically, *un*derinvest in what is comfortable (i.e., incremental improvements to existing processes, products, and services), and overinvest to an *un*comfortable degree in what could be feasible in the future.

I can't tell you what percentage of your budget you should be investing in innovative new products and services, but if it doesn't make you and your chief financial officer a little *un*comfortable, it's not enough.

Ironically, economic recessions and depressions can be good times to start new businesses. Did you know that Disney, General Electric, and Hewlett-Packard (HP) were all started during the Great Depression? Microsoft was launched during the recession of 1975, and Uber, Airbnb, and Twitter were all initiated during the economic crisis of 2008–2009.

Push into your discomfort zone!

# UNUSUAL TIP 6
## REVIST THE EIFFEL TOWER

When it was first created, the Eiffel Tower was panned as a monstrosity by critics and citizens alike. Today, it is one of the world's most iconic and popular tourist destinations. It is worth remembering this: The more *un*usual and original an idea is, the fewer people there are who can offer constructive advice and criticism.

In other words, people frequently don't even know what they will like until after they have seen it, and even then, sometimes it takes some time for people to "acquire the taste" of the original creator. Always remember: Fortune favors the bold!

# AHA #7:
## EMBRACE *UN*CERTAINTY

un *certainty*

PAST    FUTURE

" I can live with doubt and uncertainty. I think it's much more interesting to live not knowing, than to have answers that might be wrong. If we only allow that, as we progress, we remain unsure, we will leave opportunities for alternatives. We will not become enthusiastic for the fact, the knowledge, the absolute truth of the day, but remain always uncertain . . . in order to make progress, one must leave the door to the unknown ajar. "

—**Richard Feynman**

## INTERNET MEMES GO VIRAL FOR A REASON:

they capture a simple truth. One of my favorites is this photo to the right. It is of a man absorbed in his smartphone at the expense of missing a beautiful sunset.

It captures a simple and, in this case, sad truth. Too often people are focused on the "urgent" at the expense of the important.

To survive in the world of tomorrow, business leaders need to lift their heads up and scan the horizon for tomorrow's big threats—and opportunities.

In addition to the next pandemic, a list of other potential threats includes the rise of authoritarian governments, political revolutions (even in the US), economic trade wars, debilitating cybersecurity attacks, a solar storm (which could knock out the electrical grid), climate change, and any number of natural or man-made disasters.

**A wealth of information creates a poverty of attention.**

—Herbert A. Simon

# AWARENESS
## THERE ARE ALWAYS MULTIPLE PERSPECTIVES

What word do you see?

Are you sure?

Turn it upside down.

There is always a different way of seeing the world.

To this point, in May of 2018, an audio clip went viral. It was the simple pronunciation of a word. What was so *un*usual was that people heard two entirely different words—either "yanny" or "laurel." Afterward, a number of publications offered a scientific rationale for why and how people in the same room could hear different names from the same sound. The exercise offered a wonderful reminder that seemingly objective things (such as a single word) can have a level of subjectivity to them. The future is no exception.

Turn the page upside down.

WHAT DO YOU SEE?

# HUMILITY
## THERE'S NO RIGHT WAY TO SEE THINGS

If you had to describe the photo on the next page, how would you do it?

Take a minute and write what you see.

I see a _____.

Americans are likely to say, "I see a tiger in a jungle."

People from Asia frequently say something along the lines of, "I see a jungle with a tiger in it."

There is no right or wrong answer. The point is this: Americans tends to focus on the individual first (the tiger) and the broader context (the jungle) second. Whereas Asians tend to focus on the context first, and the individual is secondary.[1]

If you don't want to be caught *un*aware by the future, lose your perspective because everyone from existing and future customers to your current and would-be competitors is likely viewing things from a perspective different than your own.

---

1 "Cultural variation in eye movements during scene perception" by Hannah Faye Chua, Julie E. Boland, and Richard E. Nisbett, *Proceedings of the National Academy of Sciences*, August 30, 2005 (Vol. 102, No. 35, pages 12,629-12,633).

# ACTION
## GET A REVERSE MENTOR

Many senior business executives are fond of claiming to have "twenty-five years of experience" in their given business or industry. Often what they have is something closer to "one year of experience repeated twenty-five times."

To gain a fresh perspective on an old industry, it helps to listen and learn from younger people. A great way to formalize this process is to get a reverse mentor—a younger person who has less experience in your industry. (What you might see as a "lack of experience" can be viewed from a different perspective as being *un*burdened by assumptions, biases, and conventional wisdom.)

As a result, you may gain a new appreciation for, or an insight into, an emerging trend or technology that could be leveraged to your advantage.

# UN USUAL TIP 7
# BEWARE OF YOUR EGO

Trace a capital *E* on your forehead.

How did you trace it? There are two ways to do it: You can trace the *E* from your perspective—but if you do this it will appear backward to people viewing you. Alternatively, you can trace it backward from your perspective so that it would appear as an *E* to others in the room.

There is no "correct" way to trace the letter on your forehead, but researchers at Northwestern University have been using the test for more than a decade to measure perspective-taking—the ability to step outside one's own experience and instead see the world from the viewpoint of an outsider.

Too often, business leaders (especially those with the largest egos) miss future opportunities because they can only see the world from their myopic perspective. Remember: The problem with being at the top isn't too much perfection. It is too little perspective.

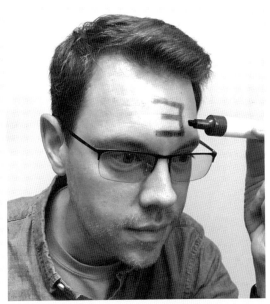

# AHA #8:
## QUESTION THE *UN*QUESTIONABLE

questionable

un

PAST     FUTURE

## LIKE MANY GOOD STORIES, THIS ONE MIGHT BE APOCRYPHAL,

but that doesn't mean it doesn't possess an element of truth. Albert Einstein was once asked this question: "If you only had an hour to solve a problem and your life depended upon getting the correct answer, how would you spend your time?"

Einstein replied: "I'd spend the first fifty-five minutes making sure I was answering the right question."

It is a wonderful response. Why? Because in today's accelerating world, future business leaders must spend more time making sure they are asking—and answering—the right question.

"In all affairs it's a healthy thing now and then to hang a question mark on the things you have long taken for granted."

—Bertrand Russell

# AWARENESS

## PRECISE ANSWERS TO THE WRONG QUESTION ARE WORTHLESS

Having the right answer to the wrong question is not only *un*helpful but also dangerous. Don't believe me? Let's just review a small list of companies that begin with the letter *B* and look at what has happened to them over the past decade: BlackBerry, Borders, and Blockbuster. They are all now bankrupt or near bankruptcy. Why? They busied themselves answering the wrong questions.

Borders didn't question how the growth of the internet might transform how books were purchased. BlackBerry didn't question how customers might interact with a smartphone in new and innovative ways. And Blockbuster didn't question the wisdom of sticking with a policy of "optimizing" revenue by charging customers late fees.

# HUMILITY
## DON'T BE WILE E. COYOTE

Picture that moment when Wile E. Coyote is chasing the Road Runner and runs off the edge of a cliff. In the cartoon, there is always that second or two where he continues to confidently run straight on thin air. Inevitably, reality sets in and Wile E. Coyote plummets to the ground.

Senior leaders at Borders, BlackBerry, and Blockbuster did much the same after a new technology or trend had taken root. They confidently kept running even though the landscape had changed.

The questions Wile E. Coyote—and all business leaders—must ask themselves are these: How has my environment changed? How soon must I stop doing what I have been doing? And how do I change course?

# CONFIDENCE IS THE FEELING BEFORE YOU UNDERSTAND THE REAL QUESTION.

# ACTION
## GIVE UP ON ANSWERS AND STICK WITH QUESTIONS

As Tony Robbins said, "Successful people ask better questions, and as a result, they get better answers."[2]

As a business leader, here's one question you should regularly ask your staff, employees, and customers: "Can you tell me something I don't want to hear?"

Others include "The Vowel" rule:

How do we need to **A**dapt?

How is our world **E**volving?

How can we **I**nnovate?

Can we **O**rganize differently?

What do we need to **U**nlearn?

Wh**Y** do we do things

the way we do them?

---

2    Tony Robbins, tonyrobbins.com/mind-meaning/ask-better-questions/.

# UNUSUAL TIP 8
# IF YOU MUST TALK, ASK QUESTIONS

Chanel, the French fashion company, has a wonderful policy for recently hired senior executives. For the first thirty days after they are hired, the executives are not allowed to speak at company meetings. The one exception is that they are allowed to ask follow-up questions.

This allows the new hires to hone their listening skills while also learning more about both the nature of the issues confronting the company and the organization's internal culture. This combination ensures that when they do speak, their insights will be sharper and their words can be chosen to achieve maximum impact.

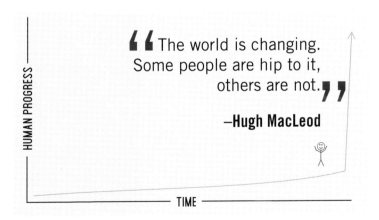

**❝The world is changing. Some people are hip to it, others are not.❞**

—Hugh MacLeod

# AHA #9:
## LISTEN TO THE *UN*CONVENTIONAL

conventional

un

PAST    FUTURE

# THE AYMARA, AN INDIGENOUS PEOPLE IN SOUTH AMERICA, HAVE A UNIQUE WAY OF THINKING ABOUT THE FUTURE.

Unlike every other culture, the Aymara refer and gesture to the future as being behind them. To our way of thinking, this is curious behavior. The Aymara's thinking, however, has an element of logic to it. From their perspective, what they can "see" is the past. Therefore, because they can see the past, it is ahead of them. What they can't see is the future; therefore, it is behind them.

There is no right or wrong way to think about—or gesture to—the future, but the anecdote serves as a reminder that if you are willing to listen to *un*conventional people, you might come to new and *un*conventional insights.

One trick for listening to *un*conventional ideas is this: Pay more attention to people who mispronounce industry jargon. Why? Because it is a sign that they have done enough reading or homework to be familiar with the term, but it also strongly suggests that they have not yet been "corrupted" by insiders who embrace "long-held" assumptions about the industry. In short, mispronunciations offer the possibility that these individuals don't hold any preconceived biases or notions about "how things are or should be."

# AWARENESS
## HEARING IS BELIEVING

Society has an implicit bias when it comes to thinking about the future. It favors sight over other senses. This bias is so strong that forward-looking individuals are hailed as visionaries and seers. But if you want to be hip to the future, strive to become a "listenary."

# HUMILITY
## DROP THE CURTAIN

Nobody ever says they are "in the process of being wrong." Instead, people say things such as "I was wrong"—with the emphasis on *was*. Or "mistakes were made" with an emphasis on *were*.

Becoming a listenary is not so much about "pulling back the curtain" on your biases and assumptions as it is about dropping it.

Until 1954, few women or minorities were members of professional orchestras across the United States. That year, one significant institutional change was made in how conductors hired professional musicians: A curtain was placed between the conductor and the auditioner. Unsurprisingly, after "blind auditions" became the norm, women and minorities were hired in larger numbers because conductors were forced to stop "listening with their eyes" and instead had to truly listen. When they did, they discovered that women and minorities were equally as accomplished as their white male counterparts.

One significant implication of this insight is it is probably time to revamp your interview and hiring processes. If you think the old "face-to-face" interview is the best way to make a final hiring decision, it's time to wake up, because the interviewer (no matter how smart, accomplished, or experienced) is the person least likely to know their own biases.

# ACTION
## HOLD AN
## "*UN*CONFERENCE"

Invite your employees to speak on any topic for five minutes. Trust that they will have some interesting things to say. Listen carefully for ideas, suggestions, and products that you or others consider *un*usual, *un*conventional, or *un*orthodox.

INSIDER                        OUTSIDER

# UNUSUAL TIP 9

# LEAD LIKE YOU'RE RIGHT, BUT LISTEN LIKE YOU'RE WRONG

General George Patton once said to his subordinates: "If everyone is thinking alike, then someone isn't thinking." In essence, he was creating a culture of candor—a culture where he not only expected, but demanded people to challenge things. Wise leaders replace "my way or the highway" commands with demands to know how—or why—they might be wrong.

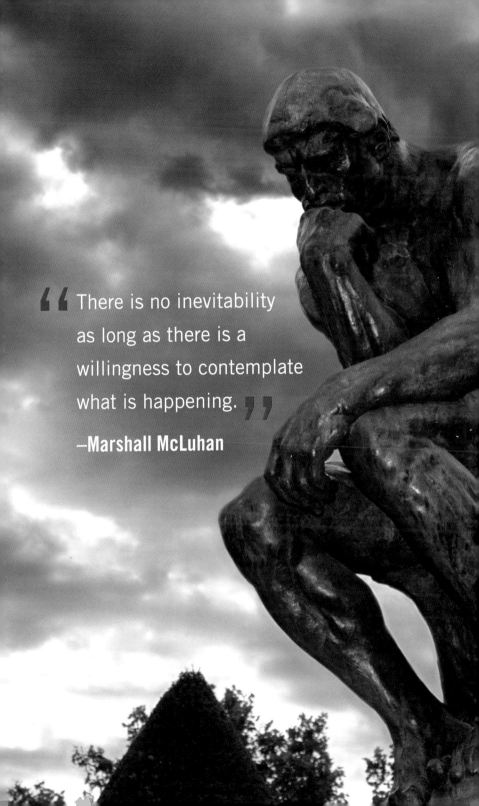

" There is no inevitability
as long as there is a
willingness to contemplate
what is happening. "

—Marshall McLuhan

# AHA #10:
## THINK THE *UN*THINKABLE

un**thinkable**

PAST     FUTURE

## AS A LEADER, YOUR TOP PRIORITY IS TO THINK.

First, think for yourself. This sounds obvious and maybe even easy to do, but know this: A person's first thought is rarely their own. More often than not, it belongs to a parent, a teacher, a coach, a professor, an old boss, or is something they have recently read in the newspaper or have seen on TV.

Next, think about the future for one simple reason—you are going to spend the rest of your life in the future.

# AWARENESS

## YOU HAVE A LOT
## TO THINK ABOUT

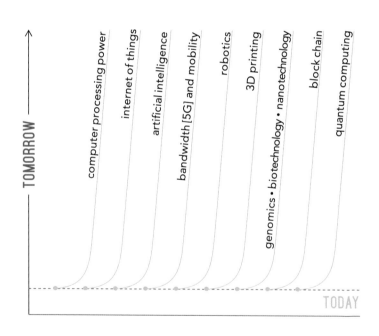

# HUMILITY
## ALWAYS THINK TWICE

Why? The answer is staring you in the face. Study the words "think twice" hard. Do you see anything else embedded in the phrase? You should.

# YOU ARE ON THIN ICE!

No matter how successful your business, no matter how *un*assailable your business model, no matter how ingrained your customers' preferences and behaviors may appear, and no matter how nonexistent competitors may seem, every business is on thin ice. So think . . . and then think twice.

Remember phase changes: At a certain temperature, ice melts into water.

It is also worth remembering that so-called once-in-a-hundred-years events don't just "happen" every hundred years—they happen frequently. This is because there is no shortage of such events and they come in a variety of different flavors—pandemics, tsunamis, hurricanes, earthquakes, wildfires, terrorist attacks, political revolutions, wars, and even "unknown unknowns." So beware!

# ACTION
## HAVE A CLOSED-DOOR POLICY

In today's business environment, it is a cliché for leaders to say they have an "open-door policy." There are real benefits to having an open-door policy, but leaders must also have a closed-door policy. Here's my advice:

Once a day (I'd suggest at 4:45 p.m.), close your door and think for fifteen minutes about how technology is advancing and how it might be leveraged to make incremental improvements to your business today.

Once a week, close your door and think for an hour about how societal, political, cultural, economic, demographic, or technological trends could alter the world of tomorrow.

Once a year, lock your office door and leave for a "think week"—ideally to a remote location with ample exposure to Mother Nature—and ruminate about the "day after tomorrow." And remember, in today's exponential world, the "day after tomorrow" will be the sum of every step of change that came before it!

Also, think long and hard about this chart:

THINK... outside the box

# UNUSUAL TIP 10
## THINK ABOUT THE *UN*THINKABLE

Every business leader should regularly conduct a "premortem" on his or her business. A premortem is the opposite of a postmortem. The purpose of the exercise is to engage in a candid conversation about the real threats to your business and business model. Instead of studying a business that went bankrupt for "lessons learned," turn the table on your business by asking your employees to imagine your company is out of business in five years. Then ask them: What didn't we see coming?

This will allow you to tap into the wisdom of your team to better explore the real threats to your business or your industry from a wider perspective. Counterintuitively, the conversation will also likely change to how a "disruption" and/or a changing world could be turned into new opportunities.

As has been said before, "The passport to a better life is to think about your death occasionally." That's good advice for both your personal life and the life of your business.

# THE FINAL AHA:
## BELIEVE THE
## *UN*BELIEVABLE

*un*believable

un

PAST    FUTURE

**I LOVE THIS PASSAGE FROM *ALICE IN WONDERLAND*. IT IS A WONDERFUL WAY TO CONCLUDE THIS BOOK.**

Alice laughed.
"One can't believe impossible things."

"I daresay you haven't had much practice," said the Queen. "When I was your age, I always did it for half-an-hour a day. Why, sometimes I've believed as many as six impossible things before breakfast."

Five hundred years ago, the earth was considered the center of the universe.

Two hundred and fifty years ago, it was widely believed that people could not govern themselves.

One hundred and twenty years ago, human flight was believed impossible by a preponderance of experts.

Fifty years ago, the notion that most people could carry an affordable supercomputer in their pocket was ludicrous.

Twenty years ago, the thought that the video game industry would be bigger than all of Hollywood was laughable.

Ten years ago, the idea that Google and Facebook would be responsible for 80 percent of all digital advertising would have been *un*imaginable.

Five years ago, the concept of businesses raising $50 billion in digital cryptocurrencies was *un*thinkable.

A year ago, a global contagion seemed implausible.

What will the world of tomorrow bring? Fusion power? Affordable quantum computers? Space travel? Two-hundred-story skyscrapers? People living to 150? Flying cars? 3D-printed human organs? Another pandemic?

Nobody knows for sure, but I do know that you must keep an open mind to the impossible!

Here's why: The sky isn't the limit.

Imagine folding a piece of paper in half over and over again. Yes, it would get smaller, but it would also get taller. How tall would the folded paper be by the fiftieth fold?

Here is the math:

10th fold: 4 inches

20th fold: the 25th floor of a skyscraper

30th fold: 62 miles, or about the height of a satellite

40th fold: the distance to the moon

50th fold: 62 million miles—or almost to the sun!

Some trends are going to double fifty times, which means that not even the sky will be the limit in the future.

Here then is my final AHA:

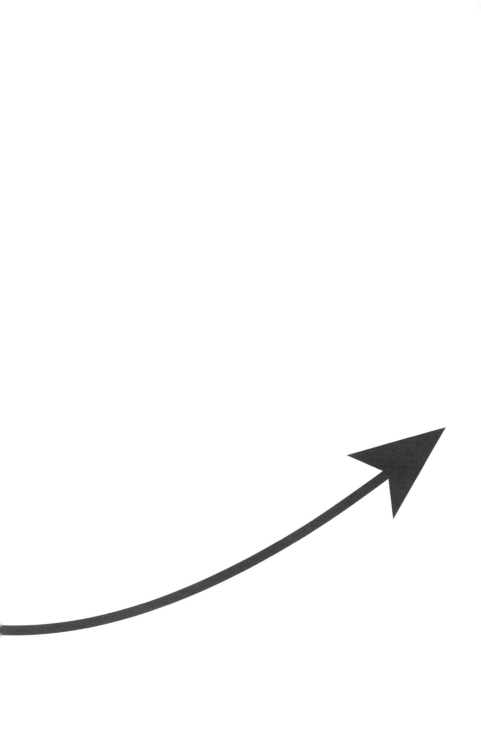

## AWARENESS

# TODAY IS THE SLOWEST RATE OF CHANGE SOCIETY WILL EVER EXPERIENCE AGAIN . . .

# HUMILITY

# THE BEST TIME TO START PREPARING FOR THE FUTURE WAS YESTERDAY . . .

# ACTION
## THE NEXT BEST TIME IS TODAY!

# FINAL *UN*USUAL TIP

## THE FUTURE IS THE ONE THING THAT EVERYONE CAN CHANGE

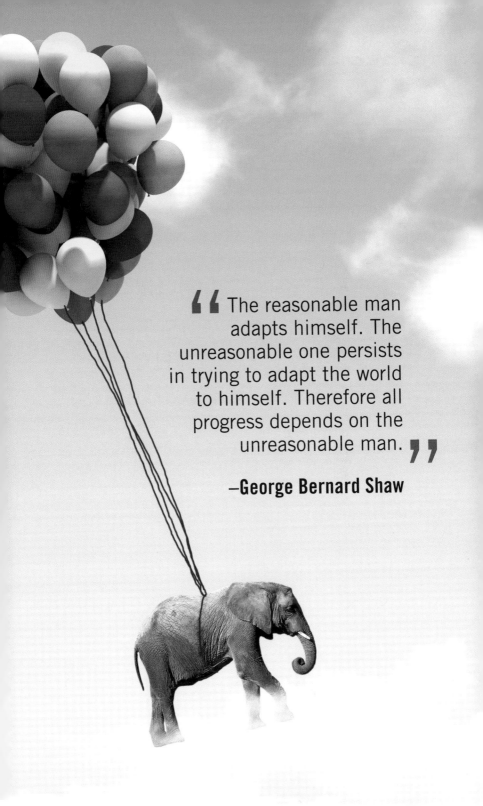

" The reasonable man adapts himself. The unreasonable one persists in trying to adapt the world to himself. Therefore all progress depends on the unreasonable man. "

—George Bernard Shaw

# APPENDIX
## JOB DESCRIPTION
## OF THE FUTURE
## (HIRE THE **UN**ORTHODOX)

Hire *un*reasonable people who:

Explore the *un*known
Search for the *un*usual
Bend *un*breakable rules
Expect the *un*expected
Entertain *un*conventional ideas
Listen to *un*orthodox thinkers
Are comfortable being *un*comfortable
Learn, *un*learn, and relearn
Play it *un*safe
Question the *un*questionable
Think the *un*thinkable, and
Believe the *un*believable.

Where do you find such people?

William Gibson said it well:

# THE **FUTURE IS HERE**, IT IS JUST NOT EVENLY DISTRIBUTED.

The future
Can often
Be found
On the




fringe.

# PHOTO CREDITS

p. 51 NYC Taxi and Limousine Commission

p. 52 Image: red background, used under license from Shutterstock.com

p. 53 Image: Alvin Toffler, used under license from Vern Evans / CC BY-SA (https://creativecommons.org/licenses/by-sa/2.0)

p. 55 Image: iceberg, used under license from Shutterstock.com

p. 56 Image: Titanic, used under license from Shutterstock.com

p. 58 Image: FedEx Registered Trademark Logo, used under license from FedEx

p. 62 Image: red background, used under license from Shutterstock.com

p. 64 Image: person doing backbend, used under license from Shutterstock.com

p. 66 Image: person diving off cliff, used under license from Shutterstock.com

p. 72 Image: red background, used under license from Shutterstock.com

p. 73 Image source "Richard Feynman" by tlwmdbt is licensed under CC BY-SA 2.0

p. 75 Image: man on beach at sunset, used under license from Shutterstock.com

p. 79 Image: tiger in jungle, used under license from Shutterstock.com

p. 84 Image: red background, used under license from Shutterstock.com

p. 86 Image: Bertrand Russell, used under license from Shutterstock.com

p. 89 Image: boy sawing off tree branch, used under license from Shutterstock.com

p. 92 Image: red background, used under license from Shutterstock.com

p. 99 Image: The Thinker, used under license from Shutterstock.com

p. 100 Image: red background, used under license from Shutterstock.com

pp. 103-104 Image: ice, used under license from Shutterstock.com

p. 108 Image: red background, used under license from Shutterstock.com

p. 110 Image: chalkboard, used under license from Shutterstock.com

p. 119 Image: elephant with balloons, used under license from Shutterstock.com

# ABOUT THE AUTHOR

**Jack Uldrich** is a leading global futurist, the bestselling author of 11 books, and a popular keynote speaker. In previous careers, he has served as a naval intelligence officer, a policy analyst for the Pentagon, and the Director of the Office of Strategic Planning for the State of Minnesota under Governor Jesse Ventura. Outside of work, he enjoys hiking, writing poems, traveling the world's rivers, and having meaningful conversations with interesting people over a good meal and glass or two of wine. He can be contacted at www.jackuldrich.com.